## MATH SMARTS!

# Data, Graphing, and Statistics

## SMARTS!

Rebecca
Wingard-Nelson

**Enslow Publishers, Inc.**
40 Industrial Road
Box 398
Berkeley Heights, NJ 07922
USA

http://www.enslow.com

Copyright © 2012 by Enslow Publishers, Inc.

Original edition published as *Data, Graphing, and Statistics* in 2004.

**Library of Congress Cataloging-in-Publication Data**

Wingard-Nelson, Rebecca.
  Data, graphing, and statistics smarts! / Rebecca Wingard-Nelson.
      p. cm. — (Math smarts!)
  Summary: "Re-inforce classroom learning of important data, graphing, and
statistics skills including circle, bar, and line graphs, scatter plots, stem-and-leaf
diagrams, mean, median, and mode, and outliers"—Provided by publisher.
  Includes index.
  ISBN 978-0-7660-3942-1
  1. Mathematics—Graphic methods—Juvenile literature. 2. Mathematics—
Charts, diagrams, etc.—Juvenile literature. 3. Mathematical statistics—Juvenile
literature.  I. Title.
  QA40.5.W56 2012
  519.5—dc22

                                                              2011008343

Paperback ISBN: 978-1-59845-323-2

Printed in China

052011 Leo Paper Group, Heshan City, Guangdong, China.

10 9 8 7 6 5 4 3 2 1

**To Our Readers:** We have done our best to make sure all Internet Addresses
in this book were active and appropriate when we went to press. However, the
author and the publisher have no control over and assume no liability for the
material available on those Internet sites or on other Web sites they may link to.
Any comments or suggestions can be sent by e-mail to comments@enslow.com
or to the address on the back cover.

**Cover Illustration:** Shutterstock.com

# Contents

# Introduction

If you were to look up the meaning of the word *mathematics*, you would find that it is the study of numbers, quantities, and shapes and how they relate to each other.

Mathematics is important to all world cultures, including our world of work. The following are just some of the ways in which studying math will help you:

▶ You will know how much money you are spending.

▶ You will know if the cashier has given you the right amount of change.

▶ You will know how to use measurements to build things.

▶ Your science classes will be easier and more interesting.

▶ You will understand music on a whole new level.

▶ You will be able to qualify for and land a rewarding job.

Statistics and graphing are important tools used every day. Data and statistics tell which radio and television shows are popular enough to stay on the air, and which should be dropped. They help us decide how much money is needed to fund agencies, and they show us trends so that we can predict what may happen next. You need to know not only how to read statistics, data, and graphs, but also how to present them effectively.

This book has been written so that you can learn about data, graphing, and statistics at your own speed. You can use this book on your own, or work together with a friend, tutor, or parent.

*Good luck and have fun!*

## Raw Data

Data is any type of information or facts. Data can be presented in different ways. Sometimes it appears as a list or table of numbers that is not organized. Other times data may be organized, like in a tally sheet. Information that has not been arranged to make it easily read and understood is called raw data.

**List**

| Birth Month of 8th – Grade Students | |
|---|---|
| January | December |
| March | March |
| February | November |
| June | June |
| March | April |
| January | May |
| August | December |
| February | June |
| July | March |
| March | June |
| September | August |
| November | June |
| December | September |
| August | April |

**Tally Sheet**

**Number of Siblings**

| 0 | 1 | 2 | 3 | Over 3 |
|---|---|---|---|---|
| $\cancel{IIII}$ II | $\cancel{IIII}$ $\cancel{IIII}$ II | $\cancel{IIII}$ $\cancel{IIII}$ | $\cancel{IIII}$ III | III |

## Organized Table

Sometimes tables are used to organize data so that the data is easier to read and understand. A table that shows how many times something has happened is called a frequency table. A frequency is the number of times something happens.

**data** — Any type of information or facts.
**graph** — A "diagram" of data.
**statistic** — A single piece of numerical information.

## Frequency Tables

| Birth Month of 8th – Grade Students | |
|---|---|
| Month | Frequency |
| January | 2 |
| February | 2 |
| March | 5 |
| April | 2 |
| May | 1 |
| June | 5 |
| July | 1 |
| August | 3 |
| September | 2 |
| October | 0 |
| November | 2 |
| December | 3 |

| Number of Siblings | Frequency |
|---|---|
| 0 | 7 |
| 1 | 12 |
| 2 | 10 |
| 3 | 8 |
| Over 3 | 3 |

You will learn how to make a frequency table in the next chapter.

## Statistics

Statistics is a type of math that deals with collecting data, organizing it, and then figuring out what it means. A statistic is a single fact, or single piece of information. Statistics are given as numbers, percentages, or ratios.

Examples of statistics:

12 of the 40 students surveyed had only one sibling.
25% of the students have two siblings.
Out of 28 eighth-grade students, none has a birthday in October.

Data may be quantitative, or have a numerical value (a quantity.) Age, height, and income are quantitative. Data may be qualitative. Qualitative data describes qualitites that are not numbers, such as color or shape.

Raw data can easily be put into a frequency table. In a frequency table, the number of times something happens is recorded as a number.

**The students in a class were asked to tell their favorite cafeteria meal. The results were recorded on the tally sheet below. Make a frequency table of the results.**

| Cheeseburger | IIII |
| Corn Dog | IIII I |
| Meatball Sub | III |
| Pizza | IIII IIII |
| Spaghetti | I |

**Step 1:** Set up a table with two columns. The first column lists the categories. The categories for this table are the type of meal. Label the columns "Meal" and "Frequency." There are five different meals, so make five rows, and write one meal in each row.

| Meal | Frequency |
|------|-----------|
| Cheeseburger | |
| Corn Dog | |
| Meatball Sub | |
| Pizza | |
| Spaghetti | |

**Step 2:** Count the number of tally marks in each meal category. Write the total for each meal in the second column.

| Meal | Frequency |
|------|-----------|
| Cheeseburger | 4 |
| Corn Dog | 6 |
| Meatball Sub | 3 |
| Pizza | 10 |
| Spaghetti | 1 |

When you are using raw data to make a graph, use a frequency table to organize the data.

# Relative Frequency Table

A relative frequency table adds one more column to a frequency table. This relative frequency column shows the frequency of the category divided by the total frequency. The relative frequency can be written as a fraction, a decimal, or a percent.

**Make a relative frequency table of the data from the cafeteria meal survey.**

**Step 1:** Find the total number of students that were surveyed by adding each category's frequency.

$$4 + 6 + 3 + 10 + 1 = 24$$

There were 24 students surveyed.

Step 2: Add a third column to the table you made on page 8. Label this column "Relative Frequency."

Step 3: Start with the first row, Cheeseburger. Divide the number of students who chose cheeseburger (4) by the total number of students (24). Write the result as a fraction and reduce the fraction to lowest terms.

number of student who chose cheeseburger $\longrightarrow$ total number of students $\longrightarrow$ $\dfrac{4}{24} = \dfrac{1}{6}$

Do this for each row. Write the fraction in the relative frequency column.

| Meal | Frequency | Relative Frequency |
|------|-----------|--------------------|
| Cheeseburger | 4 | $\dfrac{4}{24} = \dfrac{1}{6}$ |
| Corn Dog | 6 | $\dfrac{6}{24} = \dfrac{1}{4}$ |
| Meatball Sub | 3 | $\dfrac{3}{24} = \dfrac{1}{8}$ |
| Pizza | 10 | $\dfrac{10}{24} = \dfrac{5}{12}$ |
| Spaghetti | 1 | $\dfrac{1}{24}$ |

When the relative frequency is given as a fraction, the fraction should be reduced to lowest terms.

Statistics are often written as ratios. A ratio is a way to compare related numbers. For example, ratios can compare two parts of a data set, or a part of the set to the whole set.

Mr. Davis has 28 students in his class.
There are 12 boys and 16 girls in the class.

The ratio of boys to girls is a comparison of two parts of a data set. The ratio can be written in three different ways.

$$\frac{12}{16}$$

12 to 16

12 : 16

The same ratio can be reduced to lowest terms by dividing both parts by the common factor 4.

$$\frac{12 \ (\div 4)}{16 \ (\div 4)} = \frac{3}{4}$$ There are three boys to every four girls.

3 : 4

3 to 4

The ratio of boys to the whole class is a comparison of part of a data set to the whole set. The words *out of* can be used in a ratio of a part to a whole. The ratio can be left as it is, or reduced.

| 12 boys out of 28 students | 3 out of 7 students are boys |
|---|---|
| $$\frac{12}{28}$$ | $$\frac{3}{7}$$ |
| 12 to 28 | 3 to 7 |
| 12 : 28 | 3 : 7 |

A ratio is a comparison of two related numbers.

A survey of 100 people who purchased treadmills six months ago found that 12 people used the treadmill only one time, but 42 people were still using the treadmill regularly.

Write the ratio of people who used the treadmill one time to the number of people who are still using the treadmill regularly in lowest terms.

**Step 1:** The ratio can be written in three ways.

$$12 \text{ to } 42$$
$$12 : 42$$
$$\frac{12}{42}$$

**Step 2:** Reduce the ratio by dividing both 12 and 42 by 6.

$$\frac{12 \div 6}{42 \div 6} = \frac{2}{7}$$

**Step 3:** Write the answer.

The ratio of people who used the treadmill one time to people who are still using the treadmill regularly is 2 to 7.

When a ratio is written as a statistic, the data must be very clearly labeled. The ratio in the example above can be written as:

For every 2 people who used the treadmill only one time, 7 are still using the treadmill regularly after six months.

Ratios can be written as fractions. Ratios are reduced by dividing both parts of the ratio by a common factor.

A percent is a ratio that compares a number to 100.

$$x\% \text{ means } \frac{x}{100}$$

% is called a percent sign.
This is read "x percent."

Ratios that compare part of a data set to the total data set can be written as percents.

Out of 100 people surveyed about their
favorite cheese:

17 prefer American cheese
9 prefer blue cheese
53 prefer cheddar cheese
21 prefer Swiss cheese

The ratio of people who prefer Swiss cheese to the total number of people surveyed is 21 to 100. This can be written as a fraction or as a percent.

$$\frac{21}{100} \text{ or } 21\%$$

As a statistic, this can be written as:

Of the people surveyed, 21% say that Swiss cheese is their favorite kind of cheese.

*Cent* means "100." A percent is a ratio that compares a number to 100 (per 100).

**Out of 50 people surveyed about their habits, 46 said that they brush their teeth every day.**

**Write the number of people who brush their teeth daily as a statistic that uses a percentage.**

**Step 1:** Write the ratio of people who brush their teeth daily to the total number of people surveyed.

$$\frac{46}{50}$$

**Step 2:** A proportion is a set of equal ratios. Write a proportion by first writing the ratio you found. Then set it equal to the ratio of a number to 100.

$$\frac{46}{50} = \frac{x}{100}$$

**Step 3:** Solve the proportion for $x$.

$$\frac{46}{50} \times \frac{x}{100}$$

Cross multiply.

$$(46)(100) = (50)x$$

Solve for $x$ by dividing both sides of the equation by 50.

$$\frac{(46)(\cancel{100}^{\,2})}{\cancel{50}_{\,1}} = \frac{\cancel{50}x}{\cancel{50}}$$

$$(46)(2) = x$$

$$92 = x$$

**Step 4:** Now you know that $\frac{46}{50} = \frac{92}{100}$, which is the same as 92%. 92% of people surveyed said that they brush their teeth every day.

A proportion is a set of equal ratios.

The bar graph uses bars to show and compare information. The height of each bar tells you the value of the information it represents.

In this graph, each bar represents a value for a particular library. The bars are separated by a space because the values are not continuous.

The interval is the amount from one line on the scale to the next. In this graph, the interval is 100.

The scale of a bar graph is like a ruler. It measures the height of each bar. The scale should begin at 0 whenever possible. This graph has a scale of 0–500.

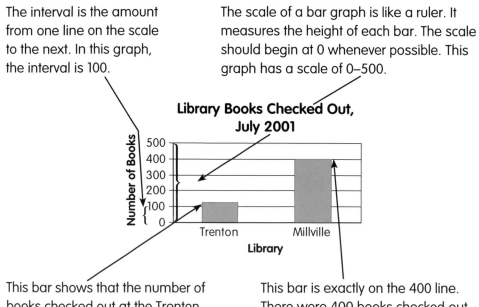

**Library Books Checked Out, July 2001**

This bar shows that the number of books checked out at the Trenton library was between 100 and 200. The bar is about $\frac{1}{4}$ of the way between 100 and 200, so a good estimate is 125 books.

This bar is exactly on the 400 line. There were 400 books checked out at the Millville library in July 2001.

**Remember:** It is important to label your graph clearly. If the values are important, you may decide to write the exact value on each bar.

**Four candidates ran for class president. The number of votes for each is in a frequency table. Make a bar graph of the data.**

| Class Election | | | |
| --- | --- | --- | --- |
| Jones | 25 | Smith | 78 |
| Wilson | 62 | Velaz | 51 |

**Step 1:** Decide on a scale and an interval. The scale must be greater than the greatest data value. A good scale for this graph would be 0 to 80.

Use an interval that the scale is easy to divide into. Since the scale goes to 80, let's use an interval of 10. Draw the interval lines.

**Step 2:** Draw a bar for each data value. Use the scale to determine the height of each bar. Be very careful to make each bar the same width, and make the spaces between bars the same.

**Step 3:** Label the axes, label and color the bars, and give the graph a title.

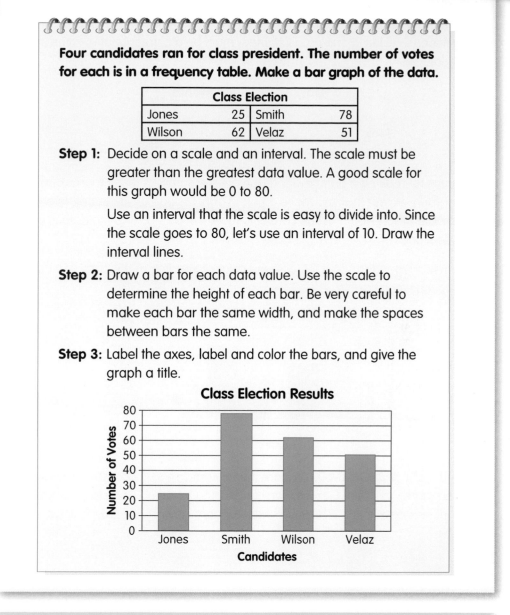

Could you have used a circle graph for the class election results? Yes! Each candidate's votes would be one section of the circle.

# Double-Bar Graphs

A double-bar graph is a special kind of bar graph that shows two sets of related data. For each value in one data set, there must be a corresponding value in the other data set.

### Days Worked per Month

|  | June | July |
|---|---|---|
| **Tony** | 20 | 22 |
| **George** | 15 | 20 |

The steps for making a double-bar graph are the same as those for making a bar graph, except that you make a pair of bars instead of single bar. In a double-bar graph, you must be careful to label the bars so that the data is easy to understand.

If you use a legend to show the different color or shading of the bars, you do not need to label each bar.

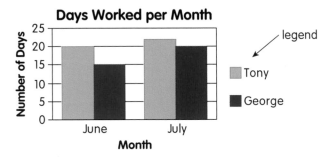

A double-bar graph lets you compare the two data sets. In both months, Tony worked more days than George. Tony and George worked close to the same amount in June and July. They both worked more days in July than in June.

Make sure to show which bar belongs with each set of data.

**Make a double-bar graph to compare the information given in the table.**

Number of Students per Sixth-Grade Class,
Divided by Gender

| Teacher | Number of Students | |
| --- | --- | --- |
| | Male | Female |
| Mr. Brown | 10 | 14 |
| Mrs. Phillips | 8 | 18 |

**Step 1:** Decide on a scale and an interval. The greatest value in either class is 18, so use a scale of 0–20. A good interval for this problem is 2, because all of the values are even numbers. Draw the interval lines.

**Step 2:** Draw the bars. The bars should be arranged in pairs, one bar from each data set. The first set of bars is for the male students. Mr. Brown has 10 and Mrs. Phillips has 8. The second set of bars is for female students. Mr. Brown has 14 and Mrs. Phillips has 18.

**Step 3:** Shade the bars and label them by assigning a shade or pattern to each set of data. Make a legend: Write the name of each class and a short example of the shade of the bar you are using for that class. You can use a lighter shade for Mr. Brown's students and a darker shade for Mrs. Phillips' students.

**Step 4:** Label the axes and give the graph a name.

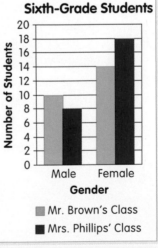

A double-bar graph is a combination of two bar graphs that have matching types of values.

A histogram is a special type of bar graph. A bar graph is a histogram only if it has certain characteristics.

The bars in a histogram are all the same width and have no spaces between them.

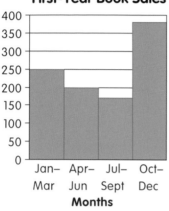

**First-Year Book Sales**

The height of each bar stands for the frequency, or number of times something happens. About 375 books were sold from October through December.

The width of each bar represents a value, like an age or a time frame, instead of a category, like gender or food group. In this graph, the bar width stands for three months.

The groups, or data that the bars stand for in a histogram, directly follow each other. For example, the first three months are directly followed by the second three months. That is why there are no spaces between the bars.

The bars in a histogram often stand for a group of values, like the months January through March, instead of one value. The group of values is called a class.

If you need more help making a bar graph, go to pages 16 and 17.

A gymnastics class kept track of the ages of its members in a table. Children under the age of 1 were recorded as 0. Make a histogram of the data.

### Class Member Ages

| | | | | |
|---|---|---|---|---|
| 3 | 1 | 3 | 8 | 8 |
| 0 | 7 | 11 | 9 | 0 |
| 2 | 4 | 0 | 2 | 3 |
| 3 | 3 | 3 | 0 | 3 |

**Step 1:** Choose a class range. Use classes that have three years in each. The first class is ages 0–2. Use tally marks to find the number of members in each age group.

| Age Range | |
|---|---|
| 0−2 | 卌 ‖ |
| 3−5 | 卌 ‖‖ |
| 6−8 | ‖‖ |
| 9−11 | ‖ |

**Step 2:** Make a frequency table from the raw data chart.

**Step 3:** Graph the range of the classes using bars that have no space between them. Label the axes and give the graph a name.

| Age Range | Frequency |
|---|---|
| 0−2 | 7 |
| 3−5 | 8 |
| 6−8 | 3 |
| 9−11 | 2 |

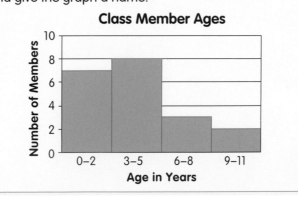

**Class Member Ages**

Often a histogram will have open-ended first or final groups, like "Over 12." This helps include small groups that have values outside the rest.

In a histogram, the frequency of each class is graphed. In the first three months, 250 books were sold, so the first bar ends at the height labeled 250.

**First-Year Book Sales**

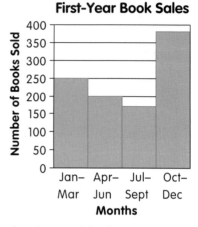

| First-Year Book Sales | | |
|---|---|---|
| Months | Number of books sold | Relative frequency |
| Jan–Mar | 250 | 0.25 |
| Apr–Jun | 200 | 0.2 |
| Jul–Sept | 170 | 0.17 |
| Oct–Dec | 380 | 0.38 |

The shape of the histogram is the same, but the scale is changed.

In a relative frequency histogram, the relative frequency is graphed instead of the actual number of books that were sold. A total of 1,000 books were sold during the first year. Of those 1,000 books, 250 were sold from January to March.

The ratio of books sold in the first three months to total books sold the first year is 250 to 1,000, or 0.25.

**First-Year Book Sales**

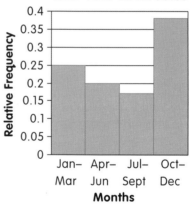

Page 9 shows how to make a relative frequency table.

Fifty employees were asked about their driving distance to work. The results were recorded in the frequency table on the right. Make a relative frequency histogram of the data.

| Driving Distance, miles | Frequency (number of people) |
|---|---|
| 0−4 | 9 |
| 5−9 | 16 |
| 10−14 | 12 |
| 15−19 | 6 |
| 20−24 | 4 |
| 25−29 | 1 |
| 30−34 | 2 |

**Step 1:** Change the frequency table to a relative frequency table. You learned about relative frequency tables in Chapter 2.

| Driving Distance | Frequency | Relative Frequency |
|---|---|---|
| 0−4 | 9 | 9/50 = 0.18 |
| 5−9 | 16 | 16/50 = 0.32 |
| 10−14 | 12 | 12/50 = 0.24 |
| 15−19 | 6 | 6/50 = 0.12 |
| 20−24 | 4 | 4/50 = 0.08 |
| 25−29 | 1 | 1/50 = 0.02 |
| 30−34 | 2 | 2/50 = 0.04 |

**Step 2:** Make a histogram using the driving distance for the horizontal axis and the relative frequency for the vertical axis. Label the axes and give the graph a title.

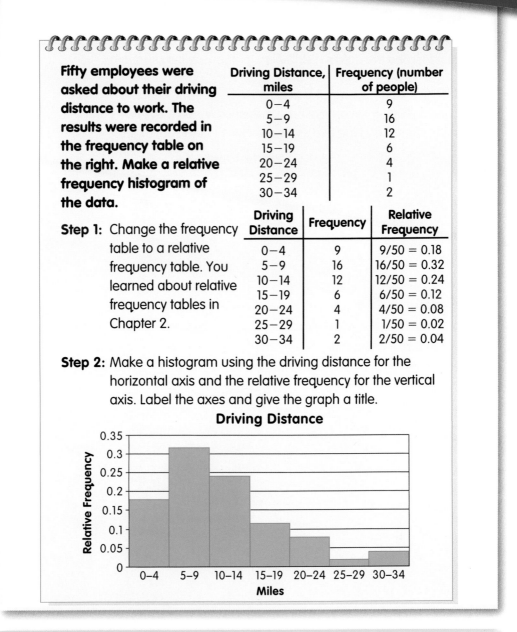

In a relative frequency table, or a relative frequency histogram, each data group is being compared to the entire data set.

Four shapes are formed when data is graphed as a histogram. The shapes are used to describe the data's distribution, or the way the data falls.

## Symmetrical

Data and its histogram are called symmetrical when the graph can be folded down the center, and the two sides are close to the same shape.

**Symmetrical**

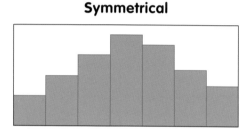

## Uniform

Uniform data has the same frequency in each category, or class. The shape of the histogram is a rectangle. A uniform histogram is symmetrical, because it can be folded down the center and the two sides are the same shape.

**Uniform**

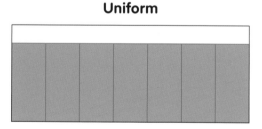

Review how to make a histogram on pages 20–21.

## Skewed

Data is skewed when the histogram has a tail that stretches out on one side more than on the other.

If the tail stretches out farther on the left, the data is skewed to the left.

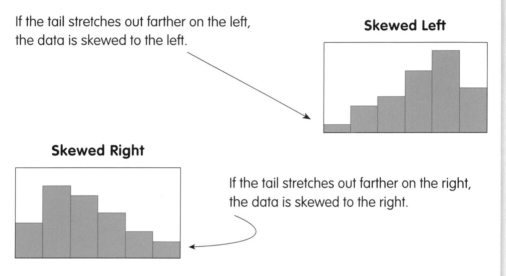

**Skewed Left**

**Skewed Right**

If the tail stretches out farther on the right, the data is skewed to the right.

## Bimodal

A histogram that has two taller bars that are separated by at least one shorter bar shows data that is bimodal.

The two taller bars will be close to the same height, but they do not need to be exactly the same.

**Bimodal**

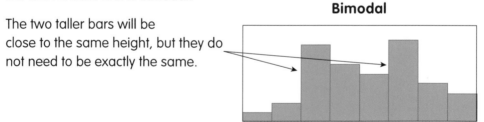

Real-world data seldom forms a perfectly shaped distribution. The distribution shapes refer to the general shape of the graph. Bimodal means "having two peaks."

Line graphs show how information changes over time. The horizontal axis shows time, plotted in equal intervals.

This line graph shows that Jim had more beef sales in later months.
In January, he only had 2 sales.
In April, he had 8 sales.

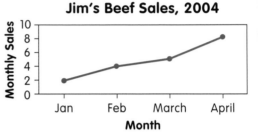

A small school club sells cases of fruit as a fund-raiser every other year. The total sales for each year are given in the frequency table below. Make a line graph of the sales.

| Fruit Club Sales | |
|---|---|
| **Year** | **Total Sales** |
| 1998 | 15 cases |
| 2000 | 35 cases |
| 2002 | 40 cases |
| 2004 | 55 cases |

**Step 1:** Decide on a scale and an interval for the *y*-axis.

The scale for the *y*-axis must be greater than the greatest data value. The greatest total was 55 cases of fruit. Use a scale of 60. Since all of the values end in a 0 or a 5, use an interval of 5.

If you have trouble reading the values for a line graph or a bar graph, you can use a ruler, a notecard, or anything with a straight edge. Line up the straight edge with the point or top of the bar, then follow it across to the *y*-axis.

**Step 2:** Draw and label the axes. Time (years) will go on the horizontal (x) axis. Label the years on the x-axis. Label only every other interval (the 10s) on the y-axis for the number of cases sold.

**Step 3:** Plot a point for each data value. Start with the first year, 1998, and the number of cases sold, 15. Find the point on the graph where a line extended from 1998 meets a line extended from the mark for 15. Draw a dot at this point. Do this for each year.

**Step 4:** Connect the points from one value to the next to form connected line segments.

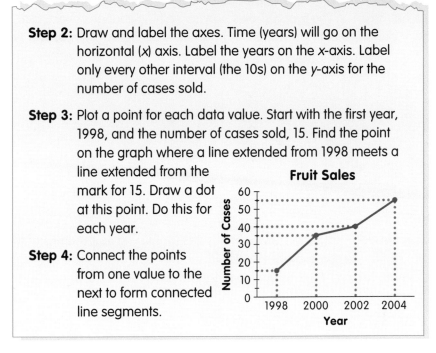

## Trends

When the line segments in a line graph show a clear direction, it is called a trend. A trend is used to predict how data may behave in the future.

Upward trend  Downward trend  Consistent trend  No trend

In the fruit sales graph, the line graph shows an upward trend, so it would be reasonable to expect that in the next sales year, more than 55 cases of fruit will be sold.

A line graph is sometimes called a time plot, because the data is graphed using consecutive equal time intervals.

A double-line graph is used to compare two sets of related data, just like a double-bar graph. A line graph shows how something changes over a period of time. A double-line graph compares how two sets of data change over time.

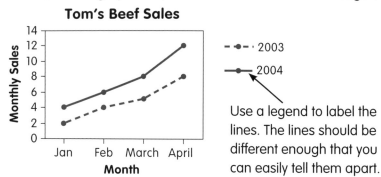

**Tom's Beef Sales**

Use a legend to label the lines. The lines should be different enough that you can easily tell them apart.

This double-line graph shows Tom's beef sales for the first four months of two different years. The graph makes it easy to see that each year the sales increase from January to April. You can also see that the sales for 2004 are greater than the sales for 2003.

In one town there are two elementary schools. The enrollment in the schools is given in the table. Compare the enrollment data in a double-line graph.

| Total Enrollment Grades K–5 | | |
| --- | --- | --- |
| School Year | Lincoln West | Lincoln Central |
| 2000–2001 | 184 | 260 |
| 2001–2002 | 234 | 240 |
| 2002–2003 | 276 | 252 |
| 2003–2004 | 290 | 236 |

The lines in a double-line graph can be different colors or different patterns. One solid line and one dotted or dashed line make a graph easy to read.

**Step 1:** Decide on a scale and an interval for the *y*-axis. The scale must be greater than the greatest data value. Use a scale of 300 and an interval of 50.

**Step 2:** Draw and label the axes. Label the graph with years and student numbers.

**Step 3:** Make a legend: Write the name of each school and a short example of the type of line you are using. You can use a solid line for Lincoln West and a dotted line for Lincoln Central.

**Step 4:** Plot the values of Lincoln West's enrollment for each year, then connect the points using a solid line.

**Step 5:** Plot the values of Lincoln Central's enrollment for each year, then connect the points using a dotted line.

**Step 6:** Give the graph a title. Make sure everything is clearly labeled.

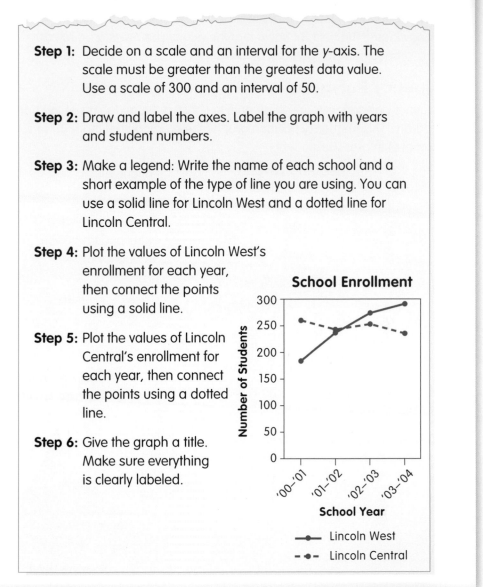

*A double-line graph shows two line graphs on the same graph.*

Sometimes when you look at a histogram, you get the idea that values jump from one class to the next. To show that the actual change is gradual, or smooth, a frequency polygon can be used.

## Frequency Polygons

A frequency polygon uses line segments to connect the midpoints of the bars in a histogram. This frequency polygon graphs the reading level (from 0.1 to 13) of a group of eighth-grade students.

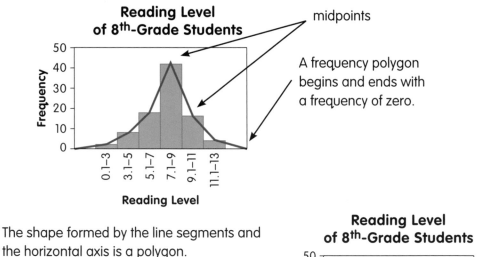

midpoints

A frequency polygon begins and ends with a frequency of zero.

The shape formed by the line segments and the horizontal axis is a polygon.

A frequency polygon is often shaded to emphasize the shape of the graph.

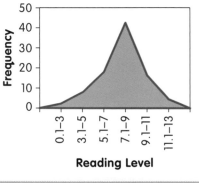

Frequency polygons can only be used for data that can be graphed in a histogram. The data must be a numerical value, like age or time, and must be continuous.

A gymnastics class kept track of the ages of its members in a table. Children under the age of 1 were recorded as 0. Make a frequency polygon of the data.

| Class Member Ages | | | | |
|---|---|---|---|---|
| 3 | 1 | 3 | 8 | 8 |
| 0 | 7 | 11 | 9 | 0 |
| 2 | 4 | 0 | 2 | 3 |
| 3 | 3 | 3 | 0 | 3 |

**Step 1:** On page 21, you made a frequency table and histogram for this problem. These were the solutions.

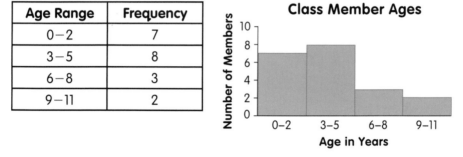

| Age Range | Frequency |
|---|---|
| 0−2 | 7 |
| 3−5 | 8 |
| 6−8 | 3 |
| 9−11 | 2 |

**Step 2:** Draw and label the axes in the same way as in the histogram.

**Step 3:** You do not need to draw the histogram. Draw a dot where the center of the top of each bar would be on the histogram. Then add a dot at zero at the left and right bottom corners of the graph.

**Step 4:** Connect the dots using line segments and shade inside the polygon.

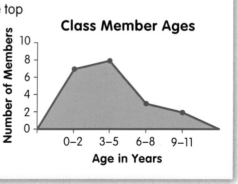

Frequency polygons are used to show the distribution of data.

## Cumulative Frequency

Cumulative means "added together." You can find the cumulative frequency of any data that can be graphed in a histogram. The cumulative frequency is the total "so far."

Reading Level of 8th-Grade Students

| Reading Level | Frequency | Cumulative Frequency |
|---|---|---|
| 0.1–3 | 2 | 2 |
| 3.1–5 | 8 | 10 |
| 5.1–7 | 18 | 28 |
| 7.1–9 | 42 | 70 |
| 9.1–11 | 16 | 86 |
| 11.1–13 | 4 | 90 |

For the first class, it is the only class "so far," so the cumulative frequency is the same as the frequency.

For each class, add to find the frequency "so far." For the reading level of 3.1–5, the cumulative frequency includes any reading level of 5 or lower. Add the frequency of reading level 0.1–3 (2) to the frequency of level 3.1–5 (8).

$$2 + 8 = 10$$

The classes must follow each other directly. There is no gap between the end value of one class and the beginning value of the next. The first class ends at a reading level of 3. The next class begins at level 3.1.

The cumulative frequency of reading level 7.1–9 is 70 students. This tells you that of 90 eighth grade students, 70 are reading at a reading level of 9 or lower.

Notice that the last cumulative frequency, 90, is the total of all the frequencies.

# Ogives

An ogive, pronounced *oh-jive*, is a graph that uses line segments to show the cumulative frequency of data.

**Graph an ogive of the reading level table on page 32.**

**Step 1:** Draw and label axes as you would in a histogram. You can use a scale of 0–100 and an interval of 10 for the vertical axis. Label the horizontal axis with the end value of each consecutive class. The first class is grade levels 0.1–3, so start with a value of 3.

**Step 2:** An ogive uses line segments to connect the endpoints of a histogram. The end of the bar is used because the whole frequency for that class is included in the cumulative frequency.

Draw a dot to show where the top of each bar would be if you were making a cumulative histogram. Add a dot at zero at the left bottom corner of the graph to show that the frequency begins at zero.

**Step 3:** Connect the dots using line segments.

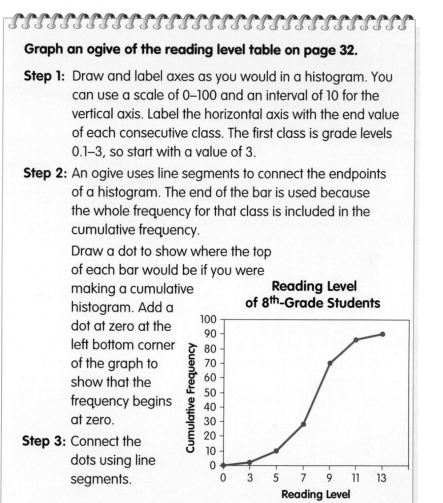

Reading Level of 8th-Grade Students

Cumulative frequency and ogives can only be found for data that is consecutive and continuous.

Some data sets are related to other data sets. Scatter plots display information in a way that makes it easier to see if there is a relationship between two sets of data.

**data set #1    data set #2**

| Outside Temp, °F | Number of People at Pool | |
|:---:|:---:|:---|
| 60 | 10 | — pair |
| 75 | 28 | — pair |
| 80 | 40 | |
| 83 | 51 | |
| 85 | 60 | |
| 90 | 75 | |

The two data sets must be in pairs. You must know which value in one set is paired with which value in the other set.

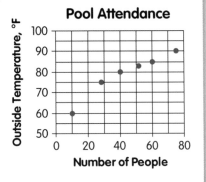

**Pool Attendance**

When the same two data sets are graphed in a scatter plot, it is easy to see that when the outside temperature goes up, pool attendance goes up. This is called a positive correlation. A negative correlation has points that show a downward trend.

Correlations may be weak or strong. A strong correlation is one in which the plotted points fall closely into a line. In a weak correlation, more points are farther from the line.

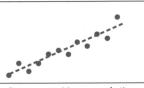

Strong positive correlation

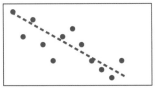

Weak negative correlation

A scatter plot, like a line graph, may be used to make predictions.

The ages and weights of children were recorded in a table. Make a scatter plot of the data. Tell if there is a correlation, and if so, what kind.

| Age in years | 6 | 6 | 7 | 7 | 8 | 9 | 9 |
|---|---|---|---|---|---|---|---|
| Weight in pounds | 48 | 62 | 50 | 70 | 74 | 72 | 88 |

**Step 1:** Each axis is used for one data set. The two data sets in the problem are age and weight. You can use the x-axis for age and the y-axis for weight.

**Step 2:** Decide on a scale and an interval for each axis. You can use a scale of 5–10 and an interval of 1 for the age axis, and a scale of 0–100 and an interval of 10 for the weight axis. Draw and label the axes.

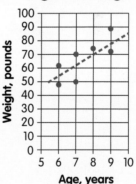

**Step 3:** Plot a point for each pair of values. Start with the first age, 6, and weight, 48. Find the point on the graph where a line extended from 6 meets a line extended from 48. Draw a dot at this point. Do this for each pair.

**Step 4:** Look at the graph to decide if there seems to be a correlation.

The points seem to form a line that goes up from left to right, so the correlation is positive. The points are not very close to the line, so the correlation is weak.

The points in a scatter plot are plotted the same way as the points in a line graph. Find the point where a line extending from an x-value meets a line extending from the corresponding y-value. Draw a dot at the point.

When the points on a scatter plot seem to fall on or near a line, it is called a linear correlation. You can sketch a line to represent the data in a scatter plot. This line is called the line of best fit. When you draw the line, there should be about the same number of points on each side of the line. The total distance from the line should be about the same for the points above as for the points below.

In some cases, the line will go through a point, or points, that you have graphed.

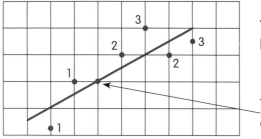

There are three points above the line and three points below the line.

This point falls on the line.

Other times, there may be a clear correlation, but there may be no data points that are exactly on the line.

There are four points above the line and four points below the line.

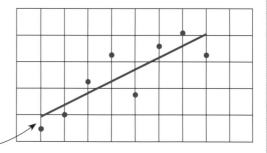

No points fall on the line.

You can find a line of best fit by looking at the scatter plot and considering each point. Sometimes there will be more points on one side of the line than on the other.

A scatter plot shows a trend, like a line graph does. The line of best fit helps you to see the trend more clearly.

**Draw a line of best fit for the following scatter plot.**

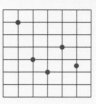

**Step 1:** Count the number of points. There are five points. The line of best fit will have about the same number of points on one side of the line as on the other.

**Step 2:** Find the type of correlation the points form. The points seem to form a negative correlation, so the line of best fit will go down from left to right.

**Step 3:** Look at the points and decide where the line of best fit belongs. Three of the points look like they will be above the line, and two will be below the line.

**Step 4:** Draw the line of best fit. The total distance of the points below the line should be about the same as the total distance of the points above the line.

One point below the line is about a unit away from the line, the other is about a unit and a half from the line, for a total of $2\frac{1}{2}$ units.

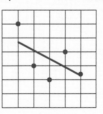

One point above the line is about a unit away from the line, the other is about a unit and a half from the line, for a total of $2\frac{1}{2}$ units. The third point is nearly on the line.

*Draw your line right through the center of the group of points.*

There are many ways you can graph the same data. Let's review the most common graphs:

**Circle graph:** In a circle graph, data is shown as parts of a circle. The circle graph shows how a whole unit, such as a budget, is divided into parts.

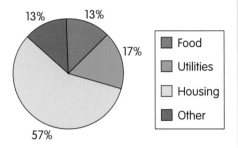

**Monthly Budget**

13%   13%   17%   57%

- Food
- Utilities
- Housing
- Other

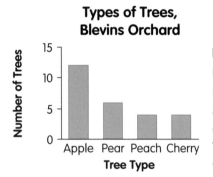

**Types of Trees, Blevins Orchard**

Number of Trees

Tree Type: Apple, Pear, Peach, Cherry

**Bar graph:** A bar graph uses bars to represent values for data. The bars can be used to compare the values. Histograms, shown on page 20, are bar graphs that use connected bars to show continuous data. The bars can be used to show a pattern or flow in the data.

**Double-bar graph:** A double-bar graph compares two sets of related data using sets of bars. Double-bar graphs must have sets of data, such as the test scores in two different schools for more than one subject.

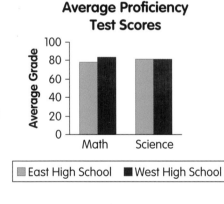

**Average Proficiency Test Scores**

Average Grade

Math   Science

- East High School
- West High School

Some data can be shown on more than one kind of graph. Check the data and the reason you are showing the data to decide which graph is the best.

**Line graph:** A line graph uses connected line segments to show how information changes over time. A line graph can show a trend in data.

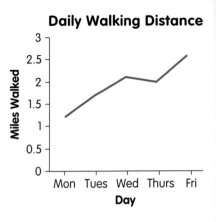

**Daily Walking Distance**

**Weekly Work Hours**

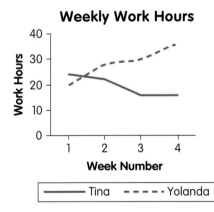

Tina — — — — Yolanda

**Double-line graph:** A double-line graph compares two sets of related data that both change over time. Double-line graphs are good for comparing trends in different sets of data.

**Scatter plot:** A scatter plot also shows how two related data sets compare to each other. It can be used to find patterns in data sets that may not seem to depend on each other.

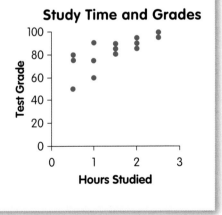

**Study Time and Grades**

Line graphs must include an axis that shows time. The time should always be divided into equal units. Bar graphs, circle graphs, and scatter plots may or may not include time.

When you are reading or making a graph, you need to be aware of how graphs can mislead the reader. One common way that a graph can be misleading is when the graph is drawn with a scale that does not begin at zero, or has a broken scale.

The graphs below show the same data. One has a scale that begins at 20 and the other has a scale that begins at 0. The interval in the first graph is 2 hours, while the second graph uses an interval of 5 hours.

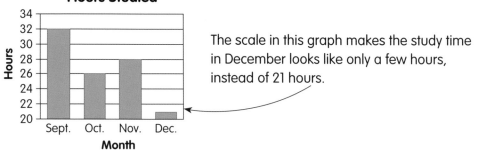

The scale in this graph makes the study time in December looks like only a few hours, instead of 21 hours.

The interval difference in the two graphs makes the change in the hours each month on the first graph appear larger than on the second graph.

You can use a broken scale when you are graphing large values that are close together. To graph the values 5,025, 5,050, and 5,100, you can use a scale that begins at 5,000. Label the scale clearly to help prevent misleading the reader.

Sometimes a graph will be misleading in order to manipulate the data and make it appear a certain way.

The next two graphs show the same data. A tall, narrow graph makes the change from one week to the next look greater than the same change looks in a short, wide graph.

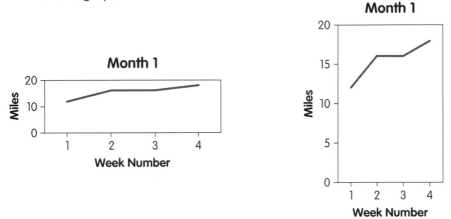

The next two graphs appear to have the same amount of growth overall if you do not carefully look at the scale and interval.

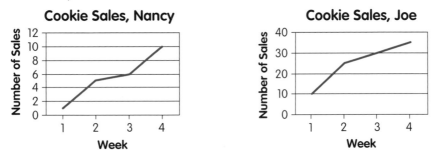

The total growth in the first graph is 9 units. The total growth in the second graph is 25 units. When two graphs are used side by side, the scales on the two graphs should be the same to prevent misleading the reader.

**Remember:** Graphs that use accurate data can still be misleading. When you are reading a graph, read the values carefully.

A line plot is a way to organize data to show how many times a value occurs and how the values are distributed. A number line and ×s are used to organize the data.

Students were tested to see how many multiplication problems they could do in one minute. Each × stands for one student.

**Number of Multiplication Problems
Finished Correctly in One Minute**

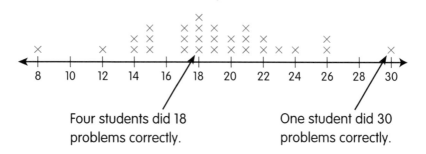

Four students did 18
problems correctly.

One student did 30
problems correctly.

The highest (30) and lowest (8) values are easy to spot. When you look at the shape formed by the ×s, you can see where most of the values fall.

A new student took the multiplication test and did 20 problems correctly. By looking at the shape of the plot, a score of 20 falls right around the center of the shape. A score of 20 is within the normal scores for the students.

A line plot shows graphically what a frequency table shows numerically.

**Strawberries are sold in one-pound containers. The raw data gives the number of berries in each container. Make a line plot of the data.**

| Number of Berries per One-Pound Container |
| --- |
| 9  12  14  15  16  17  22  10  13  14  17  18  15 |
| 16  16  17  12  13  14  15  16  18  13  10  19 |

**Step 1:** Draw a number line. The line must include the lowest and highest values. The lowest value is 9 and the highest is 22.

Choose an interval that is easy to work with and contains all of the data points. Use an interval of one unit for this data.

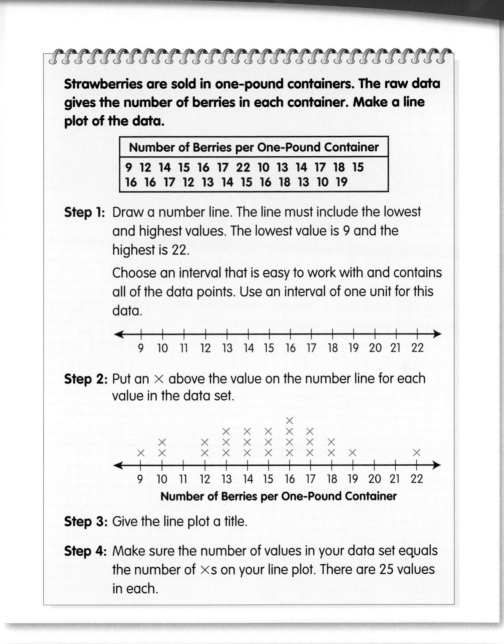

**Step 2:** Put an × above the value on the number line for each value in the data set.

**Number of Berries per One-Pound Container**

**Step 3:** Give the line plot a title.

**Step 4:** Make sure the number of values in your data set equals the number of ×s on your line plot. There are 25 values in each.

The units on a line plot number line do not have to be 1. If you choose to use a different unit, make sure you leave enough room to plot the values that fall between the units.

A stem-and-leaf diagram is used to show the frequency and distribution of the values in a data set. The leaf part of a stem-and-leaf diagram is the ones digit of each value. The stem part show the other digits. For one-digit numbers, use a zero for the stem.

The table below shows how different values are separated in a stem-and-leaf diagram.

| Value | Stem | Leaf |
| --- | --- | --- |
| 8 | 0 | 8 |
| 27 | 2 | 7 |
| 112 | 11 | 2 |
| 207 | 20 | 7 |

Each value in the data set is divided into two parts, the stem and the leaf. The value 83 is written as a stem of 8 and a leaf of 3.

The stems are separated from the leaves by a vertical line.

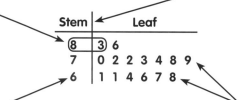

Stems are listed in a column with the largest value at the top and the smallest at the bottom.

The stem-and-leaf diagram shows that most of the values are in the 60s and 70s.

Stem-and-leaf diagrams divide the data values into multiples of 10. The longest set of leaves tells in which group of multiples of 10 most of the values fall.

Maria has a quiz every day in her math class. Her scores for this grading period are:

100 100 75 94 92 65 90 68 80

98 72 80 86 88 90 92 100 95

78 100 96 80 96 98 99 76 100

**Make a stem-and-leaf diagram of Maria's quiz scores and write a sentence describing what the diagram shows.**

**Step 1:** List the stems in a column, largest to smallest.

**Step 2:** Separate each value into a stem and a leaf. The ones digit in each value is the leaf. The rest is the stem. List the leaves beside their stems.

| Stem | Leaf |
|------|------|
| 10 | 0 0 0 0 0 |
| 9 | 4 2 0 8 0 2 5 6 6 8 9 |
| 8 | 0 0 6 8 0 |
| 7 | 5 2 8 6 |
| 6 | 5 8 |

**Step 3:** Look at the diagram. The longest set of leaves shows that most of the values are in the 90s. It is safe to say that Maria most often gets a quiz grade that is in the 90s.

Stem-and-leaf diagrams are used to find the general frequency and distribution. The value with the highest frequency is not shown.

Graphs and diagrams that show the values in a data set make it easy to see where most of the values fall. You can tell if a given value is normal, or average.

John is in a downhill ski class with 11 other students. The ages of the other students are shown in the stem-and-leaf diagram.

| Stem | Leaf |
|------|-----------|
| 4 | 1 9 |
| 3 | 1 2 3 5 6 |
| 2 | 6 7 7 |
| 1 | 9 |

John is 34 years old. He wants to know if his age is typical of the group he is in. By looking at the diagram, you can see that most of the ages fall in the 30s, so John's age is typical of the group.

## Central Tendency

Sometimes you want to know a single number to describe the entire group of data. There are three measures of central tendency, or numbers around which the data set centers.

The mean is the average of all of the values in a set of data.

The median is the center number in a set of data when the values are put in numerical order.

The mode is the value in a set of data that happens the most frequently.

---

**mean** — Average value of a data set, written as $\bar{x}$.
**median** — Middle value of a set of data.
**mode** — Most common value in a set of data.

# Mean

The mean of a set of data is often called the average. Mean is the most common measurement used to describe a data set. The mean is found by adding all of the data values together and then dividing by the number of values.

**Find the mean age of the students in John's ski class. Include John's age in the data.**

**Step 1:** Add all of the ages together.

$$19 + 26 + 27 + 27 + 31 + 32 + 33 + 34 + 35 + 36 + 41 + 49 = 390$$

**Step 2:** Find the total number of students. There were 11 students, and John makes 12.

**Step 3:** Divide the total of the ages by the total number of students.

$$390 \div 12 = 32.5$$

The mean, or average, age of the students is 32.5 years.

The mean of a data set includes every value in the set to find an average. One very small or very large number can make a significant difference in the mean.

*Just one score of zero can really bring my average down!*

Be careful to count each value, even zeros, when you are finding the mean of a data set.

The median and mode of a data set can give a better description of the set than the mean when there are one or two numbers that are far from the other values.

## Median

The median of a data set is the number that is in the middle when all of the values are put in numerical order.

**Find the median age of the students in John's ski class. Do not include John's age in the data.**

| Stem | Leaf |
|------|------|
| 4 | 1 9 |
| 3 | 1 2 3 5 6 |
| 2 | 6 7 7 |
| 1 | 9 |

**Step 1:** Put the ages of the students in order from youngest to oldest.

19 26 27 27 31 ③② 33 35 36 41 49

**Step 2:** Find the value that is in the middle. This is the median. There should be the same number of values on each side of the median.

The median age of the class is 32.

When John's age (34) is not included in the class, there is an odd number of students. If there is an even number of values, there is no value that is in the middle.

The median of a data set does not have to be a value that is in the data set. If the number of values is even, the median may be the average of the two center values.

The middle of the data set is between the ages 32 and 33.

19 26 27 27 31 32 33 34 35 36 41 49

To find the median for an even numbered data set, average the two values that are on each side of the median. The average of 32 and 33 is 32.5, because $(32 + 33) \div 2 = 65 \div 2 = 32.5$.

The median age of the group when John's age is included is 32.5 years.

## Mode

The mode of a data set is the value that occurs the most often. The mode is the best description of a data set when many of the values in the set are the exact same value.

**Find the mode of the ages of the students in John's ski class. Include John's age in the data.**

**Step 1:** List the ages of the students in numerical order.

19 26 27 27 31 32 33 34 35 36 41 49

**Step 2:** Look at the data and find any values that are listed more than one time. The value that occurs the most is the mode.

The only value that occurs more than one time is 27.

The mode of the ages is 27 years.

Data sets can have any number of modes. More than one value may occur with the highest frequency. In the ski class problem, if another student were 34, the modes of the ages would be 27 and 34, because these numbers would both occur two times.

If all of the values happen with the same frequency, the data set has no mode.

*The mean, median, and mode can all be called typical values for a collection of data.*

Sometimes when you want to average numbers, you want one of the numbers to have more importance than the other numbers. A weighted mean gives more importance to some data values than to others.

The mean of two scores, 100 and 70, is found by adding them together, then dividing by 2. The average of the two scores is 85.

$$100 + 70 = 170$$
$$170 \div 2 = 85$$

Let's say that tests are worth twice as much as quizzes. If the score of 100 is a test grade, and the 70 is a quiz, then the 100 has twice as much value.

Multiply the 100 by 2, and the 70 by 1. The 2 and 1 are the weights, or value, of each score. You must divide by the total of the weights (2 + 1 = 3). The weighted average is 90.

$$(2)100 + (1)70 = 270$$
$$270 \div 3 = 90$$

In a biology class, your final grade is made up of 10 points of homework, 20 points of quiz scores, 20 points for the midterm exam, and 50 points for the final exam grade. Each is worth 100 points. You have a 100 on your homework, an 80 on quiz grades, a 72 midterm exam grade, and a 94 final exam grade. Find your final grade for the class.

A weighted mean gives more importance to some values and less importance to others.

**Step 1:** Make a table to keep your information organized. Use a column for the grade and a column for the weight of the grade. Add a column for the product of the value times the weight.

**Step 2:** Fill in the values in the table. Multiply each value by its weight to fill in the final column.

|  | value (x) | weight (w) | (x)(w) |
|---|---|---|---|
| homework | 100 | 10 | 1,000 |
| quiz grades | 80 | 20 | 1,600 |
| midterm | 72 | 20 | 1,440 |
| final | 94 | 50 | 4,700 |
| | sum | 100 | 8,740 |

**Step 3:** Find the sum of the weights and the sum of the values multiplied by the weights. The sum of the weights is 100 and the sum of the values multiplied by their weights is 8,740.

**Step 4:** Divide the sum of each weighted value by the sum of the weights.

$$\frac{8,740}{100} = 87.4$$

Your final grade for biology is 87.4.

Hey, I can do this! The table makes it easy!

The most common use for a weighted mean is for an overall class grade.

The median of a data set divides the data into two equal parts, the lower half and the upper half.

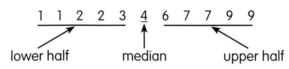

lower half       median       upper half

Quartiles, pronounced *kwor-tiles,* divide the data again, this time into four equal sections, by finding the median of each half.

## Quartiles

The lower quartile, called $Q_1$, is the median of the lower half of the data set. All of the values that are below the median are used to find the lower quartile. The median is not included when you are finding the quartiles.

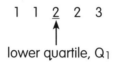

lower quartile, $Q_1$

The upper quartile, called $Q_3$, is the median of the upper half of the data set.

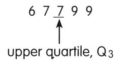

upper quartile, $Q_3$

Quartiles are the medians of the lower half and the upper half of the data set.

When a data set is divided into quartiles, the median itself is a quartile, $Q_2$.

$$1 \ 1 \ \underline{2} \ 2 \ 3 \ \underline{4} \ 6 \ 7 \ \underline{7} \ 9 \ 9$$

$$\uparrow \qquad \uparrow \qquad \uparrow$$
$$Q_1 \qquad Q_2 \qquad Q_3$$

The data now is divided into four equal sections. These sections are called quartiles.

## Interquartiles

The values that begin just after the lower quartile ($Q_1$) and end just before the upper quartile ($Q_3$) are called the interquartile. The interquartile is the middle half of the data.

$$1 \ 1 \ \underline{2} \ | \ 2 \ 3 \ \underline{4} \ 6 \ 7 \ | \ \underline{7} \ 9 \ 9$$
$$\llcorner \text{interquartile} \lrcorner$$

> *Each quartile contains about one fourth, or one quarter, of the values in the set.*

Quartiles and the median are determined by the position instead of the value of the data.

Using a number line, a box-and-whiskers plot locates five numbers to describe a data set. These numbers are the three quartiles, the lowest value, and the highest value of the set.

A box shows the middle half, or interquartile, of the data set. The box extends from the lower quartile, 2, to the upper quartile, 7. A solid line dividing the box from top to bottom shows the median, 4.

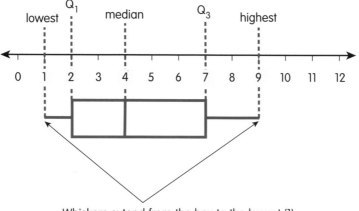

Whiskers extend from the box to the lowest (1)
and highest (9) values of the data set.

Each section of a box-and-whiskers plot represents the same number of values. When a section is shorter than another section, it shows that those values have a higher frequency.

The values in the lower whisker have a higher frequency than the values in the higher whisker, so the lower whisker is shorter.

A box-and-whiskers plot shows how the data spreads out around the median.

Make a box-and-whiskers plot for the number of points Teri has scored per game in her last fifteen basketball games. The points she scored per game are below.

30, 22, 26, 20, 18, 34, 26, 14, 22, 40, 34, 36, 45, 42, 40

**Step 1:** Put the values in order, then find the median and the quartiles.

14  18  20  22  22  26  26  30  34  34  36  40  40  42  45

       Q₁              median              Q₃

**Step 2:** Draw a number line that includes the highest (45) and lowest (14) data value. You can choose an interval other than 1 for your number line if there is a big difference between the highest and lowest data value. You can use an interval of 2 for this data set.

**Step 3:** Below the number line, draw a box from the lower quartile (22) to the upper quartile (40).

**Step 4:** Draw a solid line through the box at the median (30).

**Step 5:** Draw a solid line from the lower quartile to the lowest value in the data set (14). Draw a second line from the upper quartile to the highest value (45) in the data set.

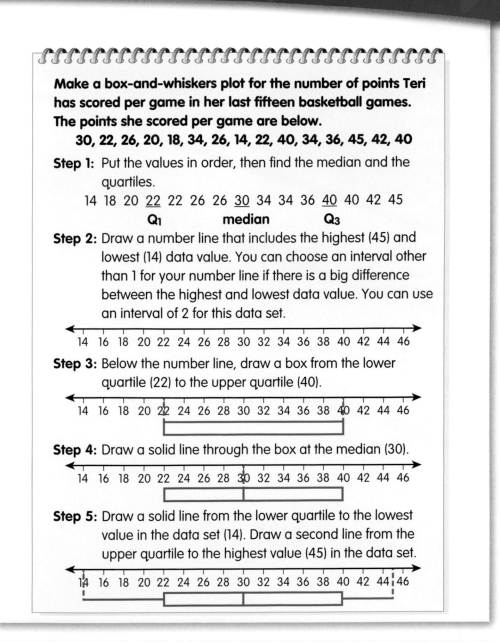

The interquartile is the data set between the lower quartile and the upper quartile.

Measures of dispersion are used to describe how data is spread out around a central value, such as the mean or median. These measurements tell how far the rest of the data set is from the mean or median.

## Range

The range of a data set is the difference between the highest data value and the lowest data value.

Take a look at the number of points Teri has scored in her last fifteen games.

$$14 \ 18 \ 20 \ \underline{22} \ 22 \ 26 \ 26 \ \underline{30} \ 34 \ 34 \ 36 \ \underline{40} \ 40 \ 42 \ 45$$
$$\quad\quad\quad\quad Q_1 \quad\quad\quad\quad\quad \text{median} \quad\quad\quad\quad Q_3$$

The least points scored were 14, and the most were 45. You can say the points scored range from 14 to 45.

$$45 - 14 = 31$$

The range of points scored is 31 points.

## IQR

The interquartile range, or IQR, is the difference between the first quartile and the third quartile. The IQR shows how the middle half of the data falls around the median. You will see how this is used in Chapter 28.

The IQR of Teri's scored points is:

$$Q_3 - Q_1 = IQR$$

$$40 - 22 = 18 \text{ points}$$

The interquartile range tells the range of the middle half of the data set.

## Mean Deviation

The mean deviation tells the average amount that the values of the data set differ from the mean.

**Find the mean deviation for the scores of five students on a science test.**

| Test scores | | | | |
|---|---|---|---|---|
| 84 | 93 | 86 | 72 | 90 |

**Step 1:** Find the mean of the test scores. Divide the sum of all the test scores by the number of test scores.

$$\frac{84 + 93 + 86 + 72 + 90}{5} = \frac{425}{5} = 85$$

The mean, $\overline{x}$, is 85.

**Step 2:** Make a table to keep your information organized. Find the absolute value of each value minus the mean.

| $x$ | $|x - \overline{x}|$ |
|---|---|
| 84 | $|84 - 85| = |-1| = 1$ |
| 93 | $|93 - 85| = |8| = 8$ |
| 86 | $|86 - 85| = |1| = 1$ |
| 72 | $|72 - 85| = |-13| = 13$ |
| 90 | $|90 - 85| = |5| = 5$ |

**Step 3:** Find the mean of the absolute values. Add the absolute values and divide by the number of values.

$$\frac{1 + 8 + 1 + 13 + 5}{5} = \frac{28}{5} = 5.6$$

The mean deviation is 5.6.

The absolute value of a number is the distance the number is from zero on a number line. The absolute value is always a positive number.

Measures of dispersion are often used to compare two or more sets of similar data, such as the rainfall of two cities over a period of time, the wear on different types of brake pads, the sizes of the blooms on two different strains of roses, or the effects of a medicine compared to the effects of a placebo.

A group of people tested a new medicine to see if it reduced the number of days a certain illness affected them. One group took the medicine, another took a placebo (a pill without any active ingredients) instead. Find the mean, range, and mean deviation of the number of days each group was affected.

| Group A – Medicine Length of Illness in Days | Group B – Placebo Length of Illness in Days |
|:---:|:---:|
| 3 | 4 |
| 1 | 5 |
| 6 | 2 |
| 5 | 4 |
| 2 | 7 |
| 1 | 3 |

**Step 1:** Find the mean of each data set.

**Group A**

$$\frac{3 + 1 + 6 + 5 + 2 + 1}{6} = \frac{18}{6} = 3$$

**Group B**

$$\frac{4 + 5 + 2 + 4 + 7 + 3}{6} = \frac{25}{6} = 4.2$$

central tendency — One number that is used to describe a set of values. The mean, median, and mode of a data set are all ways to describe central tendency. Look at pages 46–47 for more information.

**Step 2:** Find the range of each data set.

| **Group A** | **Group B** |
| :---: | :---: |
| $6 - 1 = 5$ | $7 - 2 = 5$ |

**Step 3:** Find the mean deviation of each data set. Use a table to stay organized.

| Group A | | Group B | |
| :---: | :---: | :---: | :---: |
| $x_i$ | $|x_i - \overline{x}|$ | $x_{ii}$ | $|x_{ii} - \overline{x}|$ |
| 3 | $|3 - 3| = 0$ | 4 | $|4 - 4.2| = 0.2$ |
| 1 | $|1 - 3| = 2$ | 5 | $|5 - 4.2| = 0.8$ |
| 6 | $|6 - 3| = 3$ | 2 | $|2 - 4.2| = 2.2$ |
| 5 | $|5 - 3| = 2$ | 4 | $|4 - 4.2| = 0.2$ |
| 2 | $|2 - 3| = 1$ | 7 | $|7 - 4.2| = 2.8$ |
| 1 | $|1 - 3| = 2$ | 3 | $|3 - 4.2| = 1.2$ |

mean deviation Group A:

$$\frac{0 + 2 + 3 + 2 + 1 + 2}{6} = \frac{10}{6} = 1.\overline{6}$$

mean deviation Group B:

$$\frac{0.2 + 0.8 + 2.2 + 0.2 + 2.8 + 1.2}{6} = \frac{7.4}{6} = 1.2$$

When you compare the dispersions, you can see that the group with the medicine had a lower average number of ill days, but the range of days for the two groups was the same. The mean deviation of the group with the medicine was higher, so the results were more spread out.

**range** — The difference between the highest and lowest values.

Sometimes a data set has values that just do not seem to belong with the rest. Data values that are much greater or much smaller than the other values are called outliers.

Outliers affect the way the data set as a whole unit behaves.

| Test Scores | | | |
|---|---|---|---|
| 20 | 70 | 80 | 90 |

The test score of 20% is an outlier in the data set of test scores because it is very far from the other test scores.

When the mean of the test scores is found without the outlier, the average is 80%.

$$\frac{70 + 80 + 90}{3} = 80$$

When the mean grade is found including the outlier, the mean drops to 65%.

$$\frac{20 + 70 + 80 + 90}{4} = 65$$

## Limits

An outlier is a data value that falls outside a set limit. There are two limits in a data set. There is an upper limit and a lower limit.

The limits of a data set are found by using the interquartile range, or IQR. The limits in a data set are 1.5 times the IQR above or below the interquartile of the data set.

To review the interquartile range, see page 56.

**Determine if there are any outliers in the data set below.**

$$1, 2, 3, 4, 4, 4, 5, 5, 6, 8, 11$$

**Step 1:** Put the values in order and find the median and quartiles.

$$1\ 2\ \underline{3}\ 4\ 4\ \underline{4}\ 5\ 5\ \underline{6}\ 8\ 11$$
$$Q_1\quad \text{median}\quad Q_3$$

**Step 2:** Find the interquartile range (IQR).

$$Q_3 - Q_1 = IQR$$
$$6 - 3 = 3$$

The interquartile range is 3.

**Step 3:** Find the limits.

The lower limit is 1.5 times the IQR below the lower quartile ($Q_1$). The lower quartile is 3, and the IQR is 3.

$1.5 \times IQR = 1.5 \times 3 = 4.5$
4.5 below 3, the lower quartile, means $3 - 4.5$, or $-1.5$

The lower limit is $-1.5$.

The upper limit is 1.5 times the IQR above the upper quartile ($Q_3$). The upper quartile is 6.

$1.5 \times IQR = 1.5 \times 3 = 4.5$
4.5 above 6, the upper quartile, means $6 + 4.5$, or 10.5

The upper limit is 10.5.

**Step 4:** Tell if there are any outliers.

The lower limit is $-1.5$. There are no values below $-1.5$. The upper limit is 10.5. The value 11 is above the upper limit.

The value 11 is an outlier for the given data set.

Any value below the lower limit or above the upper limit in a data set is called an outlier.

# Further Reading

## Books

Edwards, C. C. *TI-89 Graphing Calculator for Dummies.* New Jersey: Wiley Publishing, Inc., 2005.

Long, Lynette. *Great Graphs and Sensational Statistics: Games and Activities That Make Math Easy and Fun.* Indianapolis: John Wiley & Sons, 2004.

Rossman, Allan J., Chance, Beth L. and Bar von Oehson., J. *Workshop Statistics: Discovery with Data and the Graphing Calculator.* New York: Key College Publishing, 2008.

## Internet Addresses

Banfill, J. *AAA Math—Percents and Ratios.* © 2000–2003.
   <http://www.aaamath.com/rat.html>

Math League Multimedia. *Using Data and Statistics.* © 1997–2001.
   <http://www.mathleague.com/help/data/data.htm>